Dedicated to:
Jeremiah, Allison, and Adelynn

I Am Kiowa

Written By Dustin Stumblingbear

Illustrated by Tokeya Waci U Richardson

Hi, I'm Dustin.

Once upon a time, I was in the 4th grade at
Schwegler Elementary School.

One day, our teacher received a call on the classroom telephone.
After she hung up, the teacher told me to report to the office.
I thought I was in trouble.

When I got to the office, my brother and mom were already there.
I asked my brother what was going on? He was as confused as I was.

Mom told us she was checking us out of school. We were going to do a presentation about being Kiowa to a class of 5th graders at Sunset Hill Elementary School. I had never done anything like this before. I trusted my mom.

At Sunset Hill Elementary School, we put on the clothes we wear when we dance at celebrations and pow-wows. The teacher introduced us to her 5th grade class.

Mom started her presentation by telling the class about our Kiowa heritage. The students excitedly listened to her talk about the Kiowa families and the different tribes we traded and had fights with.

Then Mom shared a Kiowa fable about a man named Saynday:

Saynday was a trickster. One day, he was walking along and he was hungry. He saw a prairie dog village. He went to them and offered to sing so the prairie dogs could dance. Saynday started drumming away and singing. The prairie dogs all came out of their homes and started to dance to Saynday's music.

The prairie dogs didn't know that when they got close to Saynday he would strike them over the head with his drumstick. Then he hid the prairie dogs behind him so the others wouldn't see.

The moral of the story is, don't be so quick to accept something free.

Southern Straight Dance Regalia

A. Eagle Feather: I was given my eagle feather when I was introduced to the arena. I will keep this feather for my entire life.

B. Bandoliers: The bandoliers are made of plastic beads. For children, the plastic beads are light weight. Adult bandoliers use bone, full metal beads, and seeds.

C. Beaded Belt: We bead on a loom and then put the finished beadwork on a weight-lifter's belt. The design is the centerpiece of all the beadwork on the regalia.

D. Deer toe soundmakers: We wear deer toes around our knees to add our own sound to the rhythm of the drum as we dance.

E. Mocassins: As children, we do not have a lot of beadwork because we will get new moscassins as we grow.

A. Otter Cap: A cap made using the face and tail of an otter. The cap is a symbol of wealth and honor. Extra decorations can include beaded or silver medallions.

B. Medicine Pouches: Every person has "talents" or what we call "medicine." We will take items from nature and put them in pouches as a symbol of our talents and medicine.

C. Eagle Fan: Fans are made from the wings or tail feathers of an eagle or other birds. The handles can be beaded, have leather fringe, or just have a cloth wrapped around the handle.

D: Staff: Male dancers often carry a weapon. I carried a staff. My staff had beadwork and small feathers that hung from the tip.

E: Leggings: Our leggings are made of cloth or wool. They keep our legs safe while in the wild brush or riding our horses.

Southern Straight Dance Regalia

With the boombox playing music, I danced the Southern Straight Style for those students.

I am telling the story of a hunt when I dance. I look to the left and to the right for signs of my quarry.

During our songs, there are 3 loud beats. These are called "honor beats". When I hear these beats, I touch the tip of my staff feathers to the ground. This signals to other Kiowa I have found signs of our prey. I then dance around this spot before looking for more signs.

After I danced by myself, we invited members of the class to participate in what we call the "Two-Step." At a pow-wow, when someone asks you to dance in the Two-Step, it is a way to show you like that person. One should always accept the invitation to dance because refusing is considered very rude.

The dance is like follow the leader. When the music starts, the couple in the lead position dances around the circle, adding different moves that everybody else down the line will copy. Everyone who wanted to join was invited to get up and dance. We all had a good time.

When our family headed out to our car, the teacher stopped us. The whole class wanted to help us put our things in our car. As they helped, they kept asking lots of questions about how we knew so much about our history, our family, our dance, and our outfits.

The class waved goodbye to us as we drove away. I felt really good about being able to share who I was with that class.

Several days later, when we got home from school, my brother checked the mail and found a big envelope in our mailbox. We were excited to see what was inside but waited until mom came home.

The envelope had "thank you" letters from every student in that class.
Each student had written what they liked most about our presentation.
All three of us were so happy to read those letters.

I am Dustin.
I am Kiowa.

Who are you?
Will you share who you are with me?

The End

Dustin, a member of the Oklahoma Kiowa tribe was born in Tucson, AZ and resides in Lawrence, Kansas. He and his family were able to share their culture with students and adults across Lawrence, Kansas, NW Minnesota and NE North Dakota. Dustin deployed twice to Iraq as part of the North Dakota National Guard. Since coming home Dustin uses his time to volunteer in his community, write books, and be a doting grandfather.

Tokeya Waci U is a member of the Oglala Lakota and Haliwa-Saponi Tribes. He was born in New York City. TK has had the ability to travel across the United States learning about his culture and sharing his art with Indigenous and non-Indigenous peoples. Tokeya Waci U graduated from Haskell Indian Nations University with a degree in Fine Arts. He sees his life calling as portraying the life experiences of Indigenous peoples in his art to strengthen and empower them. You can find his art at: www.coupcountdesignz.com.

ISBN: 979-8-218-49495-7

Library of Congress Control Number: 2024917421

Published by: Cymbolz LLC
                PO Box 73
                Lawrence, KS 66044